THE DISTANCE ANYWHERE

THE LAMONT POETRY SELECTION FOR 1966
OF THE ACADEMY OF AMERICAN POETS
This distinguished award, sponsored "for the discovery
and encouragement of new poetic genius," is made every year
to an American poet who has not yet had a book of
poetry published. The judges for 1966 were
James Dickey, Anthony Hecht, William E. Stafford,
May Swenson, and James Wright.

The
Distance
Anywhere

KENNETH O. HANSON

UNIVERSITY OF WASHINGTON PRESS
SEATTLE AND LONDON

Copyright © 1967 by the University of Washington Press
Library of Congress Catalog Card Number 67–13113
Printed in the United States of America

ACKNOWLEDGMENTS

Acknowledgments are due to the following periodicals in whose pages some of these poems originally appeared: *Botteghe Oscure* (Rome), *Colorado Review, Contact, December, Embryo, Experiment, Inland, Massachusetts Review, Oregon Signatures, Poetry Northwest, San Francisco Review, Sewanee Review, Transatlantic Review.* The following poems appeared originally in *The New Yorker:* "Portrait," copyright 1953; and "Equestrian in Jalisco," copyright 1954. Some of the poems appear also in *Five Poets of the Pacific Northwest,* edited by Robin Skelton (Seattle: University of Washington Press, 1964).

CONTENTS

Part Three
HOLDING ACTION

Part Four
MAKING THE SCENE

Part One

POEMS FROM PHALERON

for Evangelos Pandos

HOTEL LIDO

After a day and a night of rain
they're cleaning up on the Saronic Gulf.
The sun burns on the water.
The doorman, dressed in dungarees
and wearing dark glasses, is shining shoes—
his smile infectious and carious.
The maid, barefooted, is cleaning out drains.
They're putting down boards on the sea-walks again.
Yesterday every place in the world
had the same bad weather.
Now, into the bright specific afternoon
the vigorous bathers come
and the dark skin-diver hangs
hours on the surface of one world
and stares into another.

SELLING FISH IN KALAMAKI

The simultaneous statement of five themes begins
—or better, six. Point, counter point,
but there resemblance ends. Along the wall
the slappy water feels the rocks.
Greeks feel each other and the fish.
The vehement gestures rise and fall
until the classic day takes place.
One Greek is beating out the life from squid.
One other bobs offshore, explaining
to himself the mustard-colored nets.
Responsibly, the opulent vocables fall on the water.
The price is set. One Greek walks off
a basket of sweet fish upon his head.

HAIRCUT ON POSEIDON STREET

I settle in, disconsolate and helpless
to this foreign barber's chair and face myself.
I'm nearer than I thought and blonder too
until I take my glasses off, and then I fade—
a fish in deeper water than the day.
The barber speaks no English and I take my chance.
What will he make of a head so long, so square
crewcut? He works in silence while I blur—
the bees in squadrons riding out the fragrant air
between the mirror and the chair.
And then the talcum drifts, I put my glasses on
and try to praise the effort honestly
that brought this self discovered to the light—
clean-cut, well-rounded, almost Greek.

A GOING CONCERN

Speeding on hair-
raising hairpin turns
through the Peloponnese
having missed
Mycenae for Messene

taking one hand
from the wheel
to cross himself
at every Dangerous Curve
my pious pimp friend
tells me Hanson be
happy. Do me the favor.

But hell what the hell
I say I don't
have to be happy I
just have to be alive.

MYCENAE

The guide says
this is the gate
Orestes came in by
this is the one
he went out
this is the secret
cistern lined
with porcelain
taking a candle
only an inch
and a half
to light us down
600 steps

Meden agan
would scarcely
be thought as
wisdom in Vermont
still they were right
the Greeks
it's the passion for more
kills enough
in a spare landscape
one learns
to remember

Against this light
that falls straight

forwardly the nerves
all sharpen them
selves like knives
and begin to sing
and tomorrow's
fortune numbered
and still clean
comes to unguarded
beaches
into every home

SWINGING IN THESSALY

Surely there are gods
in this landscape
surely
Olympos is all inhabited

shepherds piping
yes truly
with flocks a black
goat with soft eyes
and sure feet

small boys
singing mimic-bouzouki
(sometimes I'm happy
but then
sometimes I'm sad)

and eating a stolen
orange
Axarídes, Athenian
out of his element
steps on the gas
past Katerini

Matter of fact
we're not much interested
in ruins he tells me
while thunder

rolls rattling the stars
in their sockets
and sunlight
footloose
falls over Thessaly
undaunted

TRUE ENOUGH WILL DO

Triantáfilos Tsaloukídes
otherwise Lakis, "Little Flower"
street Tripóleos
played the horses
and lost his last shirt button.

My friend—it was always
my friend—I need 600 drachmas.
My mother she
very christianity, he said.
Last night she hospital.
I smoke and I smoke
(holding up his stained fingers).

O my friend
it was skilled snow job
and both of us knew it.
Now six months later
your mother long since forgotten
along with 600 drachmas
into a world where all the horses win
your letter (postage due)
comes saying, I send you letter
but you dint send me any answer.

AFTER ARCHILOCHOS

The mind delights
in one thing
after another

but Dog take your
limping iambics
Triantáfilos there's more

to life than poetry
and it's always
your friends you've

got to watch out for
your enemies can
take care of themselves

HUNG OVER IN TZITZIFIES

Completely without resources
my head splits like an orange.

In dozens of stony gardens
gardeners are gardening.
Construction workers
are working on their constructions.
Fisherman fish
and the traffic cops
are arresting pedestrians.

It is a flawless day
a day without angles.

In Phaleron Bay
with units of the 6th Fleet
the world's largest ship
the *Enterprise* idles.
"Mesa se mia nikta" [1]
rises from a thousand motorcycles.
"Den pirázi" [2] echoes
in the sleep of a hundred pimps.
All over Athens
women in black
are hanging out laundry

[1] A well-known *bouzouki* song. Roughly: "Our love affair / turned my hair / white overnight. / Why do you do me this way?"
[2] Another well-known song. Roughly: "Relax. Take it easy. Doesn't matter. Don't give it a second thought."

white as the sides of houses.
The fish hang suspended
under the glassy waves.

Completely without resources
my head splits like an orange.

Sponge salesmen sing
"very fine, very nice."
On beaches, the paddleball
players play
by the loud-sounding sea.
Just over this balcony
jet planes turn left or turn right
for Paris or Munich
or London non-stop.
On Rodos, old men on donkeys
are raising their hats
to the passing drivers.
Commuters are changing
for Metamorphosis.
Anemones blossom.
The cards fall right.

It is a flawless day
a day without angles.

Completely without resources
my head splits like an orange.

TAKE IT FROM ME

Plain truth would never serve
not Axarídes. The goddam Greeks
he'd say are a no good people.
You gotta be careful—
a line I'd heard somewhere before
and slowly I got the picture.

I have beautiful eyes for see with
he said almost running down
the bandoleered policeman outside Megalópolis.
Why don't you drive like an American I said.
These village people are stupid he said.
They don't know the tomb of Agamemnon.
Neither did he.

One time I had a fever he said
my mother she took me to a witch
who cut my tongue.
You take me to this witch I said
I'd like to know.
She's outside Phársala he said.

In Phársala then it was *halvas*
we gotta have *halvas*.
Too sweet I said. I don't like sweet.
But it's something we gotta *do* he said
so we stopped and he got six boxes

one for his mother his sister his cousin his girl
and two for him. My money of course.

Greeks never fill the tank he said
so I pushed the car uphill
round a mountain curve at midnight
down into Lárissa.
You stick with me he said
and I stuck, through Argos and Lindos
Lárissa, Phársala and Megalópolis.
It seemed like a month of Sundays
neurasthenics falling from all the olive trees
and the late king coming and going
along Poseidon Street on his way to the airport.

That was the winter
I watched them knocking the old house down.
The Athens News said wolves
ranged the villages in Thessaly.
Friends said the swans on the Thames
were dying by thousands.
You stick with me he said
I'll teach you thinking like a Greek
and I got the picture—pure *paramythy*
nothing but the best and me to pay.
I was the land of opportunity.

But look at it my way.
Here was a new geography
a mind where anything that grows

grows by a kind of tour de force
requiring only unconditional surrender.
Here was the pure perfection of an art.
Nothing like it in the British Museum.

SPEAKING OF LANGUAGE

Nothing is real
to the mind of a Greek
without endless discussion.

The Acropolis
is nothing but pure explanation.
Everywhere peddlers

with bright carts argue
the prices of oranges
round as vowels.

Sunion has Lord
Byron's initials in marble.
In Kallithea nightly

Costa, best dancer
won't till provoked
by language. Then too

there is Yorgo
who was last year
a girl till the hospital

changed him. Ask him
how it goes. Nothing
convincing stays

unless touched by language.
These are examples.
These are a few

examples—clear
light and the gritty soil
of an endless discussion.

Part Two

THE DISTANCE ANYWHERE

TWO LOOK AT THE LAKE

Across the lake the masts of racing boats
descend, stretched thin through this apparent
metal to their solid grave. Along the shore
the willows are tall shivers in the wind
before the light falls, anchoring the sky.

Whatever frames the scene—Poussin, the cat
stretched on the sill—is all peripheral.
The poem lies somewhere between. And yet
somehow the scene is not the same for you,
the cat is not this cat, but brings a memory
of other summers, childhood, maiden aunts.

Behind the mirror of the lake, your boats
are motionless, remote, until the scene
is like a postcard. Even the willows change,
are somehow "more poetic," and the light
when it comes, to the wakening of birds,
comes with profounder thunder, not like it comes.

STATISTIC

This is the scene exactly as it was,
the ruined flies on the windowledge,
damp coffee grounds, a knife, a rose
from the wall, clogging the sink.
Two bulbs burned in the sockets of brass claws.
This is the scene exactly as it was.

The papers tell how she hated her mother,
arranged the kill, hid, sat in the cold flat,
hearing the harbor whistles. There
with her lover the abstract Kid
she watched the rose on the wall repeat,
a day and a day. He didn't return,
Persephone tearing the fairytale to shreds
like a handkerchief. There's nothing more.

She set her wild blood free on its course,
she stopped it cold in its tracks.
When the bills ran up, she cut her closest ties.
Time, for a little time after she died,
chirped like a cricket tied to her wrist.

PORTRAIT

Perhaps the meticulous photographer
was a stranger, asking you to stand
(try to look natural) against
the obviously painted scene, one hand
placed casually on your vest
next to what must have been
a gold watch chain. You chose to lean
half carelessly against the plaster
tree trunk, facing the camera
on the obviously planned occasion
as if you managed to exist
only by a kind of perpetual contest.
Try to look natural. Reflect
on the day, the wedding or reunion.
Who am I that you should stare
so grimly from a world the color
of old ivory or amber, your hair
parted with a dark precision
your eyes bright as trinkets for
barter, cold as ponds in winter
and empty of love as a tin cup
in the hands of a beggar?

INTERIOR

These things are round: the wheel
where this woman seems to spin,
staring at fields outside the window,
the rug where a cat is curled in
the geometric center, these few
copper pots and a dark platter.
Everything else is strict with corners.
The light where it enters the window
is flat, the color of butter, and the sea
if there is a sea beyond the fields
is perfectly flat. From the picture
it is difficult to imagine that the wheel
has ever turned, or that the woman
looking beyond the fields could ever
guess the rummage of the sea, or that
this light could shine too on the fierce
intricate tropics, or the sun like butter
could burn itself down to a cinder
or ever be anything but round.

BEFORE THE STORM

One summer, high in Wyoming
we drove nine miles and paid
to see the great whale, pickled
and hauled on a flatcar crosscountry.
"Throat no bigger'n a orange,"
the man said, in a smell to high
heaven. I wondered how Jonah
could weather that rubbery household
tangled in fish six fathoms down.
Now, beached by the sun and
shunted to a siding, the gray
beast lay dissolving in chains.

It was none of my business
late in the day, while overhead
Stars and Stripes Forever played
in a national breeze, to sidle
past ropes and poke with a ginger
finger, nostril and lip and eye
till Hey! said the man, keep away
from my whale! But too late,
too late. I had made my mark.
The eye in its liquid socket swung,
the jaw clanged shut, and all the way home
through the bone-dry gullies I could
hear the heart as big as a bushel

beat. O weeks I went drowned
while red-winged grasshoppers span
like flying fish, and the mile-high
weather gathered its forces.

THE CROSSING

Indifferent to the light
which changed midway

her bent bones preceded
by a straight stick she

crossed the intersection
while traffic waited

and she told herself
wholeheartedly some

winding story, neither
defeated nor kowtowing

as could be seen by
that blossom, black

plastic on a thin stem
she wore like a miner's

headlamp, facing into
the hard sun, defiant.

MOTORCYCLISTS

How I envy the confident
easy performers, at home
on the road, who move
as if daddy owned stock
in the company, speak
their lines carelessly
never at a loss, who
know from the first what
their part and the name
of the play is and die
when they do, wherever
they are, boots on, arms
and legs every which way,
themselves to the very end.

EQUESTRIAN IN JALISCO

Dark eyed, the children stare
from doorways of white houses
where shopworn pigeons are
cooing on all the roofs.

Staring, they watch the soldier
ride into the burnished square,
ride up to the pink cathedral
frosted with flowery saints
like a great rococo cake
and dismount with a jingle.

In another minute he will speak
and they will vanish forever
mysterious as flights of birds.
And in the cavernous silence
the polished dust will drift

where the soldier, mounted again
on his black horse, holds a classic pose
forever in the empty square
and bound in hoops of iron
slowly his cold eyes burn.

ON A DEAD CAT IN MEXICO

Here lies what the quick body
has become—old bag of bones, mere
carpentry, a congress for all the flies
on Calle de Pepe Llano nearly.

Paws with their scimitars stretch
in a sunlight thick and unscrupulous
while fiestas of children chant
after me: " '*Allo cinco,* '*Allo money!*"

Toltec, Tarascan, Indian faces
with the eyes of raptorial birds,
and nowhere the sign of a personal loss
for the gray cat scrawny as cactus,
gone like a minor civic virtue.

SAN MIGUEL DE ALLENDE

Again this morning, American painters
are painting the church in the plaza.
The teacher is saying, "To catch the light
's the trick. Dutch light is domestic,
French is a plant that grows too green.
This light lacks all direction, falls
like a bundle of sticks, or is southern,
watery, and flows." They peer at the church
through the watery southern light
while the morning goes on around them.

Cicadas are giving an edge to the air
as Ezequiel Torres, *chine* boy, greets *"El avion!"*
the drunk at 11 A.M., weaving beautifully,
like a butterfly, toward the cage of the Cucaracha,
and mustachioed police with squirt guns
are annihilating fleas in the six local taxis.

O what will the ladies from Punxsatawney,
Twin Lakes, or Drain, Oregon, keep
of this morning so filled with implacable
foreign birds? Will they remember the slicker
hawking his magical root cure-all
in the market, the rain saint chanted
with crosses and thorns uphill to Querétaro
and every day opening with burros and bells?

Perhaps. But always when the northern season
turns anfractuous and spare, against the bells
and the flies and the kite in the distance
they will hear the voice of the instructor
praising the canvas that came between them and the
     scene
and bore the innocent truths of art, the church
in a wobbly line, and Ezequiel in spite of himself
home through customs, into a light solid as stone.

GETTING A SHINE ON THE GINZA

Remembering later
how they bow
how the waiter
stood
how the conductor
took off his cap
I think
there is room
for a garden
anywhere—

"The bean curd
bakes over char
coal flaming like
lotus blossoms"

or take bamboo—
to bend
is not necessarily
to give in

ONE AT THE E MOON

Six weeks and two typhoons away,
beached in a foreign bar
whose name has no meaning,
molding like Sidney Greenstreet from
some rash or a tropical fungus,
I try to concentrate on
the text for today.
"The sage delights in water,
the poet takes to the hills."

Outside this air-conditioned time
a garden repeats the scroll
and I watch the elegant waterfall
fall past what seem to be
the mountains of Kweilin.
There are blank spaces on the wall.

On the wall, the lizard moves
with the rhythm of an early movie.
Twin joys. *Shuang Hsi.*
The plum wine blossoms and I hear
somewhere under the rocks and the water
the sound of a world slowly turning.
What is empty? What is full? Only
the four corners of the past stand pat.

ENTRANCE INTO THE CITY

Dogs at the gates of day
with vigorous alarm forecast
all strangers. From towers
on the hour the tall clocks
ring to please themselves—
clang clang, a flattering gift
for the brazen doves.

Elsewhere in the listing city
crowds rich as timothy
grow on streetcorners, stand
motionless, bend to the rumors,
expect from a cloudless sky
the pronouncement of carnivals.
Maps in a number of colors
report the selection of streets
they are likely to come by.

For days in the dark museums
curious schoolchildren
flourishing voices like pincers
have filed past the kings in cases,
learning to recognize and name
masters of vast desert kingdoms
still stretching somewhere
under a lemon sun.

When finally they appear—
the chiming acrobats, lions
with violent manes, the captives
chained or in cages, and the long
columns of soldiers (some selling
their colored maps and looking
quite lifelike)—the children
who have all been taught three ways
to tell the true from the false dead
explode with flowers, "hurrah! hurrah!"
and the crowds set like clocks
to expect kings with curly beards
only pretend to be disappointed.

Later, in the comfortable suburbs
old men weep on picket fences,
crying "Time! O cruel season!"
This too they pretend
not to enjoy. And in the park
where the dogs of summer
drowse in pavilions of parasols
the colorful children are already
translating into dull history
their lost, holy wars.

SIDESHOW

Under the weight of souvenirs,
the paper lei, the monkey on a stick
we hear the summer gathered in a spiel.
Such wonders crowd our common place!
Such grim perfection of astounding skill!
We envy the deft magicians who produce
soiled handkerchiefs from the pure air,
wince at the crabbed proportions of a dwarf,
doubt stubbornly the dog-faced boy.
This is the mummy, imperfect now,
a hole where his sawdust innards spill.
No sign of viscera. We stare unmoved.

Like Simon simple to the fair we pass
the last cash barrier to seek our fortune
in the cards, discount the future
witnessed by our hand (a change of scene,
new friends, perhaps a violent end),
peer at the wrenching mirrors where
we're patched parsed withered & askew,
our vast head dandled on a stalk
so sprung our very name hangs loose.

How shall we greet these prodigies
who share no Africa, observe no past?
who wear no saving motto blazed
above the ineradicable heart?
Disjoined, hand arm & eye at odds,

we stand exhibited before these cold
observers like an awkward guest.
When shall our crooked kingdom come,
our cracked & elementary bones construct
their sole authentic skeleton?

Blind lights annoy the vacant air
where possibilities by life grown large
prevent the gaudy miracle to join
this audience, to read our fortune
quartered in the knavish mirrors, back
into the patient deck. We wait.
Behind the tent a cricket chirrs.
Torn posters scatter on the walk.
The moon has vanished like a palmer's coin.
We stiffen, hesitate, turn back.
Beyond the park, the gypsies & the clowns
are changing in the silent dark.

ELEGIAC

Morning this morning wakes me
to April, nostalgia, insouciant
season, whose importance
like the ambition of the Romans
is chiefly historical. I
remember Quinn's, where fat Sylvia
tended bar, bleached blond;

the beer was rich, the glasses full
and Spring came staggering up the hill
to light with his riot forsythia,
the flowering plum on 42nd,
and expire in a thirst at the door.
Loggers, householders, a renegade
scholar: *numero deus impare gaudet*:

what a bunch a characters, Quinn
said, very Roman, who one day tired
of dice, music, good fellowship
and gave his name to a fishmarket
in the north end of town, a change
the world widely ignored. O
this morning I think of it sadly.

THE DISTANCE ANYWHERE

My neighbor, a lady from Fu-kien
has rearranged her yard completely.
She has cut down the willow tree,
burning it, piecemeal, against a city
ordinance, and has put in its place
her garden of strange herbs.

I confess I resent the diligence
her side of the fence—the stink
of that oriental spinach she hangs
on the clothesline to dry, and the squawk
of the chicken I suspect she keeps,
against a city ordinance, shut up
in the white garage, eventual soup.

But when, across the rows of what-
ever she grows, she brings her
fabulous speech to bear, birds
in the trees, the very butterflies
unbend, acknowledging, to syllables
of that exacter scale, she'd make
the neighborhood, the unaccustomed
air, for all the world to see,
sight, sound and smell, Fu-kien,
beyond our ordinances, clear.

Part Three

HOLDING ACTION

THE PROVINCES

Between his "On the one hand
on the other" grows
the pied magician's rose.
Bare stage, three objects, so.
A matter of technique.

We praise the skill
although we know his every trick—
pure gesture whose repose
from the astonished wire
brings forth a practiced rose
and then the curtain falls.

We say the meaning lies beyond.
In that dead silence backstage,
stripped of tricks, the best
magician must become himself
the rose unblossom
and the crew go home.

Cramped in his gesture,
poised like a dancer
days and weeks while
endlessly the curtain falls—
we say the stage magician knows
himself the product of the act,
a skilled rehearsal of the rose.

Why should his own good time
bring down the house?
Why should he choose applause?
Worn petals on a wire—
this fraud we understand.

Did not the melancholy rose
for all its daring dew depend
on that deceitful stem,
what would we make of him
whose every night the curtain rises
on perfect surprises?

VIVALDI AT HIGH TIDE

for B. and D. H.

Discovered while the calendar
was running out, good fortune
means the catch we're partial to,
Magnolia: a bluff, where twice a day
around the house, the moon brings in
what it can of the sea, and Tuesday's
banana boat sails by on schedule.

Magnificently solvent, the sea
brings bottled messages (Rejoice!)
four kinds of gulls and a horned grebe.
They flourish in windows big
as all outdoors, and the planets spin.
Across the floor, past witnesses,
the perishing daylight falls

unarmed. So much hath time
concealed remembrances from those
who figure in its changing scenes,
we say this time of year put cats
in the rafters, gulls on the rock,
hold your breath long enough
all the world will turn wizard.

We win from the daylight handily,
and the sea comes and goes.

WEST GREENLANDERS

                    who
kept the stone age going
north of Thule, dueled
in public to a hand drum
while they sang their
rich obscenities in rime
impromptu, turn by turn.
He won who proved most
master of abuse. O
useful muse! To please
that small community
and win your case! They
needed every man where
life came not more com-
plicated than the primrose
and the gnat, until one
day religion and a Danish
rifle shocked them up
to date, and primrose
gnat their stone age arctic
indiscreet and skillful
roundabout, died out.

NOOTKA

In the old days
Mrs Annie or Doctor
Long Tom rich
with fish could
sing to the beat
of a rattling drum
"I am trying to look
as pretty as I can
because my lover
is in the crowd."

Or changing the beat
"I'd have cut off
his head and carried
it through town,
except it would
have had such a
crying expression."

Now in a duplex
across the street
Tom Brandon, nine
is practicing scales
an opening wedge
into the morning.
Doctor Long Tom
is dead. The Nootka
singing has ended.

And they say a woman
in New Mexico has
been elected chief
of the Mescalero.

THE GAME

Autochthonous, beneath
the moon, they seek that
element or act, their
private hemisphere—

       —the clown
whose face behind the mask
repeats the mask

       —deep fish
whose headlights, thin
galvanic lanterns hung
(how Japanese) on slender
threads provoke the sea's
dark festival

       —asleep,
the ferret whose clockwork
wise to the falconer
wears his bells, so kept
so pocketed he shares
the hare's blind future

       —and the hawk
whose glamor hides rich
boredom; knows what pinned
aloft he'll prove; who
skilled may cheat the hare's

bleak waywarding, display
his fear, yet fail
(so mastered by the part)
that other's pure
                disinterest.

HOLDING ACTION

My landlord's sons
called Marky and Bobby
built a snowman once
when the dead winter sky
dropped a glittering white
all over the city
and nobody had chains
and school stopped cold.

Four days it stood
controlling the landscape
till Monday the sun
came out and Marky
in red boots—a south-
western cowboy whose
perilous nature marched
with a draggle of flag

round the melting bird-
bath and up to the pear tree
and back—bright scenery
shifting everywhere—
and drawing a bead
on the difficult season
he moved to a springtime
likelier than most

his turning world four
square in my window, borne
on the back of a turtle
as the Buddhists say.

DIMENSION

for Tot

Memory changes it slightly, moves
this to the right and that to the left
keeps the light too long or takes it

too soon. Birds on their gaudy branches
sing "June will not come again." Our
shadows flirt and fall on the green.

We swim through plangent air toward an
impossible past, mapped fish to our
landlocked home, free as a mirror is.

RIDING SHOTGUN

1

Reading Bill Stafford's book
which came out late
and taking its own sweet time

—into that common world
signed vividly by night
"Yankee go home"

or "Tony is the one for me"
comes transcontinental
one of the toughs.

The sun, round present, brings
all Kansas plain—a center
till (the phone gone dead)

"I miss Miss Kitty"
huskily, thin birds
on a wire sing.

2

Surrounded by nearness
all things respond

and dazed while the world
swings wide and out
we hear if we listen

beyond that word
as charming as candor, truth

holed-up in a stubborn landscape
our baby-faced killer.

ONE NIGHT

with Manuel Izquierdo
talking to Tomasito
the scab, the strikebreaker
though I only
found this out later

I first saw him as
the dark lady killer
white teeth, thin mustache
who kept saying Man
I don't dig your sculpture
and buying the beer

which made me wonder
till I found out he'd
married a fast blond
with 2 kids—a big house
a big car—and what
can you do most places

a Mexican

SOME TIMES FOR A SMALL SONG

1 Spring

The black cat has folded
himself on his knees
under the apple tree.

Blossoms are falling.
One has fallen on his nose.
He is a tiger in Mozambique.

He ignores the postman
passing. Come, cat
quiet as a kumquat. There

are no tigers in Mozambique.
The postman is passing.
Blossoms are falling.

2 for Gertrude Stein

Fifty persons
can be a collection
of one. One

collects seven.
That's easier even.
Fifty persons

can easily be.
Faithfully yours.

3   for Ichiro Ogha ("Dr. Lotus")
Your delicate
machines prove

the lotus blossoms
in absolute silence.

Yet in a thousand
poems I hear it

quietly open.

4   Against the Grain
Ammianus's teeth
are golden, his nails
and his navel are golden
and his limbs have been
sweetened with spices.

Petals of the chaste
lotus have been inserted
into his penis, and his
cold brains pulled out
through his nostrils.

Thus have his relatives
arranged, that in death
as in life he will move
only in the best circles.

5   Protocol

:or to say with the cat
(bright Apollo
brought down
to his tin pan)
"I prefer an
elegant simplicity"

Say, "This night
breeds crickets"

or "Walls (waltz)
a glisten of bottles
in stone"

       Sometimes
a thing can be made
too clear.

THE LARKING

"There are no true skylarks in America"

One
damn
bird
on a limb by the window
bangs the drum early
morning after morning

one
damn
bird
with a rowdy tune
too wheat oodle tweet
too lewdly starts
and the rest join

O racketeer!
assassin of sleep!
Big Noise!
You break the locks
you start the clocks
what's in it for you?

One
bird

   "April in Fairbanks"

"Jammin' the Blues"

THE SOUND OF THE FOLLOWING MUSIC

Consider a moment not
the state of our race in space
but what follows us down the street
a boy on a bike, one gray-faced dog
with a bark like the squeal of brakes.

This June morning in Portland
population 385,000
all the children age 9 to 12
are bicycling to music lessons—
violin, trombone, snare drums
glockenspiel, flute, recorder, kazoo—
scales fall from their lips and fingers
like rain as they barrel along.

Think of John Philip Sousa
Phillip Emanuel Bach, Villa-Lobos
and Julia Ward Howe—what
would they care for a man on the moon
for bundles of barbed wire flung
through the atmosphere, taking its bloodcount?
What would they say about
"O sole mio" played in concert
overtures to the morning, filling the windy spaces
what would they say about so much music
enclosed in black cases, carried along
in a bicycle basket, boy on a bike
one gray-faced dog, going somewhere to happen?

DIVISIONS ON A CRITICAL GROUND

The principal food of the tiger in India
is cattle, deer, wildhog and pea-fowl, and
occasionally human beings.

Encyclopaedia Britannica, 11th ed., Vol. XXVI ("Sub to Tom"), p. 967

1

Observe the chaste expression
and the wild career:

above the plain, each tiger
on a central pin
breakneck assaults the air
and breakneck stops,
as if all tigers moved the same.

And though surprised he feels
likewise compelled by wheels
the drab rhinoceros
in tin-plate moves
the way the tiger does.

Strange similarity.
We call it "the unity of art."

2

And see, these birds, all different.
They cannot sing

without the cage
whose tuned machinery
provides the key.

And though the cages seem
about the same, the birds
when properly adjusted
all sing different songs
like real birds.

We call this "the variety of art."

3

Tigers belong
to maharajahs solely.
Rhinoceroses, though fierce,
are fiercely melancholy.

Locked in the summer air
among green ordinary trees,
green birds in a gather
sing, sing, sweetly.

GOODBYE FOR BEING RIGHT

Having read once in
The National Geographic
"Who for the Soochow Ho"
(*ho* being river)
and having admired
that resonance

—having observed
during World War II
spun flat across Texas
a country hit tune
called "Iwo Jima's Isle"
(*jima* being isle)

—and having further
heard the Fox (being old Ez)
in a remarkable cadence
tell us who "with
herds and with cohorts
looked on Mt. Taishan"
(*shan* being mountain)

I bring these instances
together, more to instruct
than to delight, more
to delight than in despair
knowing that everywhere

war or no war
the geographers are always
right, and the poets
when they try to put space
around words are brought
to a blankness

—the floating island
holds in the distance as
the imperial mountain holds
and the wide world opens
arid and bright and clear
faced with a silence.

Part Four

MAKING THE SCENE

(after Lin Ho-ching)

Lin Ho-ching was an eleventh-century Sung dynasty poet. He was a great drinker, frequently falling on his face at the conclusion of a poem. He refused to work or to write for the government, and preferred to live at West Lake and raise cranes. Ho-ching was the name given him by a later Emperor, T'ien Sheng, and it means "the peaceful and quiet one."

SPRING

Surrounded by
anything growing
I stop and think.

The crane stands
on one leg among
lilies. The bees go

bumbling in and out
of the flowers.
Wine slows me down.

I poke and prod
at the roots of things
and remember

too late how fond
the painters were
of stairs that lead nowhere.

\

PUT IT THIS WAY

The big news
walks only
down main street

not here
where the alders mark
time to a local

breeze moving
over the fishpond.
"Ni hao ma"

I drink
to the late afternoon
as woodsmoke

rises, blue
over green roofs
and the day

time birds come back
bringing
news of the sunset.

HERE AND NOW

Winter-spring-daily
the house gets lonelier.
The big spruce shuts
out the world so completely
I welcome even weather
from the Gulf of Alaska
like an old friend.

Every morning the mirror
reflects more clearly
my withering sameness.
And though I pledge
a health to my health
nothing changes—the blood
thins out, the heart slows
loving only the landscape.

IN A GREEN LANDSCAPE

In April the clear pond
thickens with live green.
Wild plum-buds
burn at the branch tips.
The grass roots quicken.
Bright birds nest.

Thus an old man rounds
the inconsequent season.
I remember those early
poets, their odes and albas—
the air full of accidents.
How should I tell where
remembering them brings me?

STONE MOUNTAIN

In rainy weather
from this lookout
the mountain seems
held by the river.

No temple roofs
angles and curves.
Only autumn green
bleaching and dull.

Always the fisherman
always the changing
pattern of gulls
as they come and go.

Who'd think some
pipsqueak official
'd dare move Li Po's tomb
from this setting?

ONE / TWO

Sumac and joint-grass
reflect on the clear pond.

Likewise the sunset.

So, as if drawn on a golden screen
two waterbirds take flight

toward one destination.

RICE FIELD

Black soil
green
rice shoots

thick water
in the roily
ditch

surely
a subject
for some

painter
the gnarled
farmer

spring
plowing

BOATING

Pale as a mirror the lake
seems a world without edges.
Trees become clouds and clouds trees
in a watery oneness.

Lured by that pure intersection—
blue hills and a stony shore—
the creek overflowing its banks
by the cabin, I tie up—

my flask of wine a fine forethought—
one with the world, for hours.

SNOW

Eight
A.M. with the doors
and windows drifted shut—
how could there be
any dust on the knobby sculpture?

The day
is as self-contained
as the life of a stylite—
pure as "Persimmons"
by Mu-ch'i.

Step
out and the sidewalks crack.
Brisk willows
don't budge in the snow.

Stone
sober this morning
I can't bear the thought
of deliberate action—not

with the world
so shined by the weather.

MORE SNOW

Last night the snow
smoothed over the landscape
not an edge is showing
neither hedges nor ditches
and cold cracked the fat
rhododendron buds.

In the morning light
the frozen canal
looks black as a cup of tea
and the ponds too.

Myself at a loss—
boxed in by the day
I take down a book
and caught by the hard
riding rhythm I see them
the armed horsemen
farther than Turkestan.

"An eagle floats by
almost touching them.

Their feet
are quite numb
in their spurs."

THE DIVIDE

I confess I get moony
when I see these
out of the way places.

Parked for a minute
I look down at
the clapboard houses.

Foot of the hill
I drink spring water
so cold my back teeth ache.

God! Childhood!
how soon I forgot it!

MONTANA

Just over the border
a handful of stores
both sides of the road—
grocery, filling station, feed store
drug store, depot, tavern.

I wait on the platform
for the one daily train south.
The vapors of summer rise over the rails
and the dust shines, north and south.
From somewhere a black dog
is going home obliquely.

After three months
I still don't much want to leave.
Every day like today—arid & flat & spare
but with beautiful small signs
as August dies.

Now there's a fat blues
spilling from the door of Ed's Happy Haven
and the neon comes on
(before night does)
seeming to say to me Don't
go   Don't go   Come back

MAKING THE SCENE

One notable critic complains
my poems don't deal
with the larger issues.

I look at Mount Pilchuck
in spring under a green rain
dripping from the eaves.

Well there are some
would put the gull down
for not wanting to be an eagle

and the lizard
for changing quick as a wink.
From where I sit

new pine-shoots glisten
over Queen Anne's lace
at the foot of the meadow

and one day last week
a guitar-playing scholar
stopped by to copy

a song from a notebook—
anxious to get
the set of the words just right.

WEST LAKE

Exuberant, restless
Nature, itself unformed
gave form to the lake
and the landscape—
distinctive as
color on plain ground.

In April the water
is jade green, clear
as a monk's eye.
Blue evening hangs
on the hills like dust
on a ripened plum.

The garfish moving
moves its shadow
on the whitewashed wall.
All things are one.
Gull's feather falls
to the fisherman's float.
Small wind. Slant rain.

Far off, the sound
of "Walkin' the Dog"

fading.

BEGINNING

Shoes echo, a sharp sound.
I hope for the best.
The bamboo clashes in the wind
like knives being sharpened.

As the moon goes
shadows move over the wall.
What a gasser this nature is—
nothing unchanged for long.

The pond darkens. Edges
fail. Night takes it all.